Monet Love-Peterson

SASHA
THE SHARING ELEPHANT

Illustrated by HadiamirFarhan

Printed in the Unted States of America
Lulu Press, Morrisville, NC

First time printing: April 2021

ISBN: 978-1-7362209-6-2

This book is dedicated to my niece Sasha Poo.

Thank you for your KIND heart and spreading love everywhere you go.
Love always, Aunt Mo

Sasha was a sweet elephant.
So joyful and kind.
She loves to share.
The best friend anyone could find.

She really loves cookies, her favorite treat.
Chocolate chip, sugar and vanilla sweet
Peanut butter, gingerbread, everything neat.

She loved to sing her song, As she traveled along.
A small mouse named Caleb Her partner all day long.
"We got 10 cookies, yeah!" "We on a roll, yeah!"
"We got 10 cookies, yeah!" "We on our stroll, yeah!"

As she danced and sang on the trail.
She saw a beautiful family of gazelles.
They were listening to her happy tune.
And asked for the cookies shaped like the moon.

"Of course I will share!"
Sharing is so much fun.
You've got to try these yummy sugary ones!

The mouse was worried.
He started doing the math.
We had ten, now there's seven.
They surely won't last!

Can we still sing our song?
Sasha said "we sure can!
Give and it will come back to you
It's God's prosperous plan.

"We got 7 cookies, yeah!"
"We on a roll, yeah!"
"We got 7 cookies, yeah!"
"We on our stroll, yeah!"

A sweet zebra and her babies
Came by the watering hole.
Heard the song of sweets
And petitioned for the treats.

"Of course I will share!"
"Sharing is so much fun."
"You've got to try these
yummy chocolate chip ones!"

The mouse was worried again. He started
doing the math. We had seven, now there's two.
My goodness they're going fast.
"We got 2 cookies, yeah!" "We on a roll, yeah!"
"We got 2 cookies, yeah!" "We on our stroll, yeah!"

Sasha says, It's okay, we have two.
And that's perfect for me and you.
But then came a pair
Of little chimpanzees.
Super silly and busy as bees. Hungry little furry pair
asking if I had cookies to spare.

They heard they were soft.
They heard they were chewy.
They wondered if she would
Share the last of them gooey.

The final two were birthday cake cookies. She knew she'd make more so she surrendered to these rookies. The two chimps were laughing, so grateful they flipped. Sweet Sasha was giving, and poor Caleb was sick.

The worrisome Caleb
Went crazy inside.
How can we celebrate?
How will we survive?

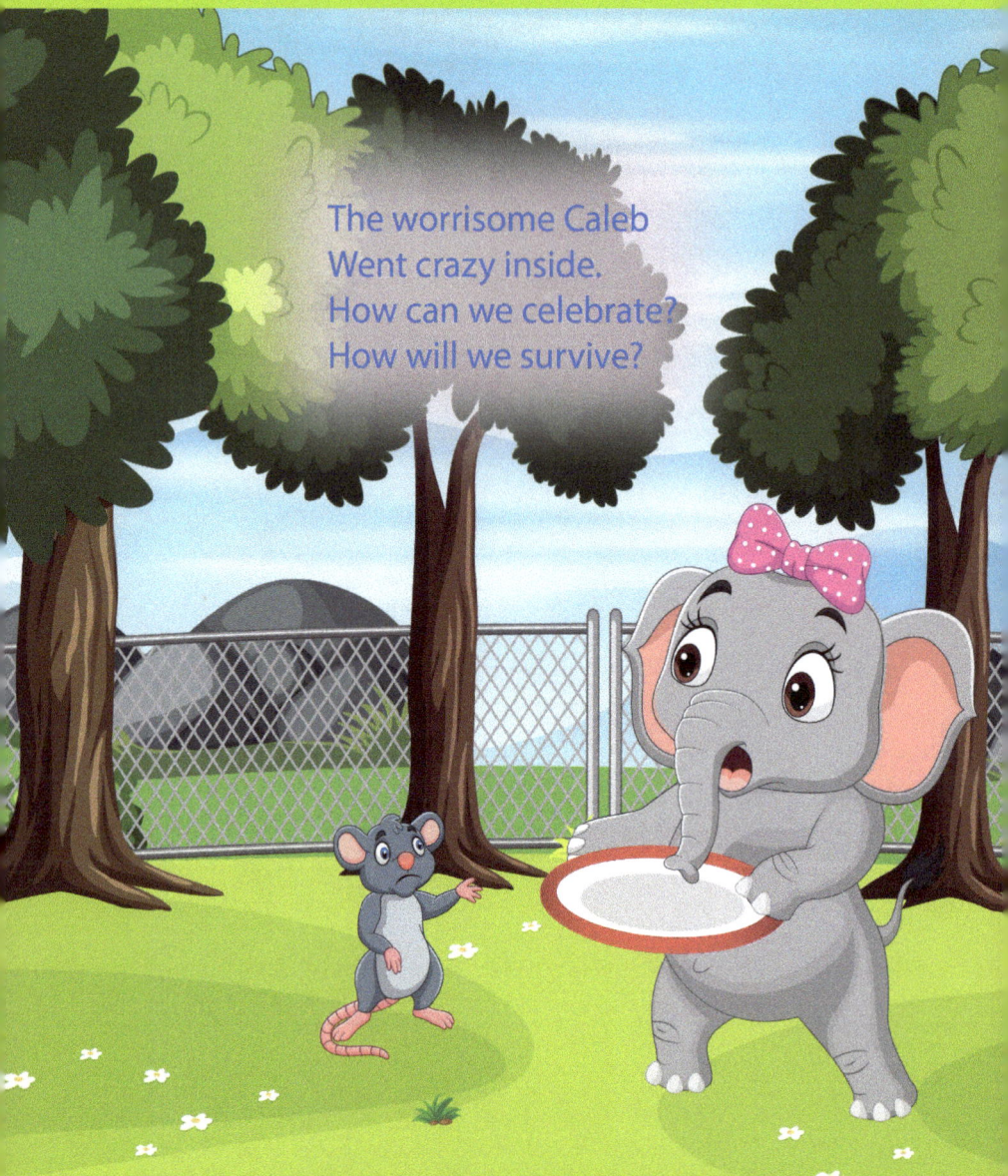

No cookies, we're done!
We can't sing our song.
It's ruined it's over!
Everything is all wrong!

But right at that moment,
Right at that minute,
The sweet happy Sister
Of Sasha was in it!

Sanaa baked and she rolled just like a machine.
She was so proud of Sasha. The cookies were presitine.

While she was giving away her treats
Her sister was planning and aiming to meet,
Meet her kindness and goodness inside.
Give her twenty for the ten she provided.

Sasha rejoiced so happy with cheer
Always give, and have no fear.
No fear to love.
No fear to give.
Sharing is caring and helps you to live.
So remember to give, no matter the cost.
Giving is easy instead of a loss.

"Give, and it will be given to you; good measure, pressed down, shaken together, and running over will be put into your bosom. For with the same measure that you use, it will be measured back to Luke 6:38

www.ingramcontent.com/pod-product-compliance
Lightning Source LLC
Chambersburg PA
CBHW051216150426
R18143100001BA/R181431PG42813CBX00007BA/1